# Artificial Intelligence Demystified: A Practical Guide for Beginners

- Musarrat Husain

# Preface

## The Human Behind the Machine

I didn't start as an AI expert. I started as a **problem-solver**.

In factories buzzing with machines, where grease met code and decisions were made in milliseconds, I watched intelligent people struggle to make sense of so-called "smart systems." Shop-floor supervisors, production managers, procurement heads — all trying to navigate through dashboards that blinked like Christmas lights but said little of value. They didn't need another tool. They needed clarity.

As someone who has spent years at the intersection of manufacturing, software, and strategy — and as the founder of Hackaback Technologies — I've witnessed firsthand how **technology, when wrapped in jargon, alienates the very people it is meant to empower**. And yet, when explained with empathy and relevance, even the most complex AI model becomes an idea you can grasp, discuss over coffee, and possibly integrate into your workflow tomorrow.

This book was born out of **conversations with engineers, business owners, students, and curious professionals** — people who felt they were being left behind in a world racing toward algorithms, agents, and automation. They didn't want to code neural networks. They just wanted to understand what the buzz was about — and how to make sense of it without a degree in computer science.

If that's you, welcome.

This is not a technical manual. It's a **narrative tour of the AI world**, told in a way that **connects AI to the human brain, a vending machine, or even a toddler learning to walk**. It's a book that believes **you don't need to be 'sharp' — just curious.** Because intelligence, both artificial and human, is nothing without the will to learn.

You'll find stories from boardrooms and shop floors, metaphors that involve dogs and thermostats, and diagrams that don't try to show off. You'll see how AI is not some magical force but a collection of very human decisions encoded in software. And by the time you reach the last page, my hope is simple: that you feel smarter, not because you memorized something, but because you understood something.

Let's demystify the machine — together.

**Musarrat Husain**

Founder & CEO, Hackaback Technologies

# Table of Contents

# Chapter 1: Introduction to AI – What and Why?

Have you ever wondered how your phone can recognize your face or how Netflix seems to *know* what show you might want to watch next? These are everyday examples of **Artificial Intelligence (AI)** at work. In simple terms, **Artificial Intelligence** is the science of making machines **smart** – enabling computers to perform tasks that would normally require human intelligencehcltech.com. This means a computer system can be programmed (or even learn on its own) to do things like understand language, recognize images, make decisions, or translate speech in real time – tasks we usually associate with human thinking iotforall.com. For instance, AI allows machines to **see** (identify objects in images), **hear and speak** (understand voice commands and respond), and **decide** (make recommendations or plans) in ways that mimic human capabilitiesibm.com.

Many people imagine AI as human-like robots from science fiction. It's true that AI was a popular topic in sci-fi long before it became reality – think of movies like *The Terminator* – which leads to a common misconception that AI means sentient robots poised to take overhcltech.com. In reality, AI today is much more about useful software behind the scenes than dramatic robot assistants. It's the **smartness** inside programs and devices that helps them perform specific tasks intelligently. AI can be *narrow*, designed for a focused job (like playing chess, driving a car, or filtering emails), as opposed to a mythical all-knowing machine.

**AI in everyday life:** AI has rapidly moved from research labs into the fabric of daily life and business. Often, we use AI without even realizing it. When you unlock your smartphone using facial recognition, an AI algorithm is analyzing your facial features to verify your identity iotforall.com. When you say, *"Hey Siri, what's the weather?"*, your virtual assistant uses AI to understand your voice and fetch the answer iotforall.com. Streaming services like Netflix or Spotify analyze your past viewing or listening habits and *intelligently* suggest what you might enjoy next – a feature powered by AI recommendation models. Even your email spam filter that keeps your inbox clean is driven by AI learned rules. Companies use AI to detect credit card fraud by noticing unusual spending patternsiotforall.com, and doctors are beginning to use AI to help analyze medical scans for diagnoses. In other words, AI is not a distant concept; it's all around you, enhancing convenience and efficiency in countless ways.

Why the buzz about AI now? In recent years, advances in computing power, availability of big data, and new techniques (like **Machine Learning**, which we'll explore soon) have led to AI systems that achieve impressive feats. AI programs have beaten world champions in complex games, driven cars autonomously, and even engage in human-like conversations. A notable example is AI chatbots like ChatGPT, which can hold conversations and answer questions in a very human-like manner – a task that was pure science fiction not long ago. Businesses across industries – finance, healthcare, retail, manufacturing, you name it – are investing in AI to improve services or gain insights. As a professional, even if you don't have a technical background, understanding AI is increasingly important. It enables you to grasp how these technologies might impact your field, how to harness them, and how to navigate the changes they bring.

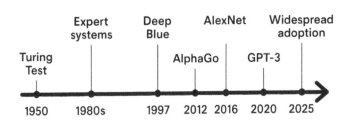

**In this book**, we'll demystify AI and its related subfields in clear, everyday language. We'll start with the basics of how machines learn from data (machine learning) using simple analogies. We'll look at common AI applications you might encounter day-to-day. Then we'll break down key concepts like supervised, unsupervised, and reinforcement learning – explaining each with real-world analogies (imagine teaching a child or training a pet). We'll introduce the idea of **AI agents** – programs or robots that perceive their environment and make decisions – and see practical examples of agents in action. Along the way, we'll include simple pseudocode (plain-English code-like steps) to illustrate how these processes work under the hood, without diving into actual programming. Finally, we'll discuss the ethical considerations and limitations of AI in a beginner-friendly way, so you're aware of both the potentials and challenges of this technology. By the end, you should have a solid understanding of what AI and ML are, how they work in principle, and how they are applied, all without the need for an engineering degree. Let's get started on this journey to understand the intelligent machines among us!

*(Summary: AI is about computers doing tasks that normally require human intelligence, from recognizing faces to making decisions [iotforall.com](iotforall.com). It's already part of daily life – in your phone, your apps, your car – often behind the scenes. Instead of thinking of sci-fi robots, it's more useful to think of AI as smart software helping with specific tasks. In the next chapters, we'll break down how AI works, especially through machine learning, using simple examples and analogies.)*

**Thought Exercise: Spotting AI**

1. List 3 daily AI interactions (e.g., GPS, streaming).

2. Guess the AI task (e.g., route prediction).

3. Discuss with a colleague.

# Chapter 2: Fundamentals of Machine Learning – How Machines Learn

To understand modern AI, we need to understand **Machine Learning (ML)**. Machine learning is essentially the engine that has driven most recent advances in AI. But what exactly is it? In a nutshell, **Machine Learning** is a subset of AI that focuses on *teaching* computers to learn from examples and data, rather than explicitly programming them with step-by-step instructionsibm.com. Instead of a human programmer writing a rigid algorithm for every scenario, the machine learning approach gives the computer a lot of data and lets it **figure out** the patterns or rules. The computer essentially *programs itself* through learning from data.

An easy way to think about this is by comparing it to how humans learn. Consider how a child learns to identify animals. You don't give the child an exhaustive list of rules for every animal ("A cat has exactly this tail length, this fur pattern, etc."). Instead, you show them lots of pictures of cats and dogs, saying which is which. Over time, the child picks up on the patterns – e.g., cats tend to have certain shapes and behaviors, dogs look different – and the child learns to tell them apart. In the future, even if the child sees a new breed of dog or cat they've never seen before, they can often still identify it by recalling those learned patterns. **Machine learning works in much the same way**: we feed the computer many examples and it learns the underlying patterns.

Let's contrast this with **traditional programming** to really drive the point home. In traditional programming, a developer writes explicit rules and logic. For example, to filter spam emails, a traditional program might have a long list of **if-then rules** (if the email contains certain keywords or comes from certain addresses, mark it as spam). The machine does exactly what it's told, nothing more. This approach can become very complex as the task complexity grows, and it's limited by the programmer's ability to foresee all scenarios. Now enter machine learning: instead of manually coding rules for filtering spam, you could provide an ML system with a large set of emails labeled as "spam" or "not spam". The machine learning algorithm will *learn* the characteristics of spam from these examples – perhaps it discovers that spam emails often have phrases like "Congratulations, you won!" or come from addresses not in your contacts. The ML model develops its own internal rules or a model based on patterns in the data. In summary, **traditional programming** is like giving a strict recipe to a computer, whereas **machine learning** is like teaching the computer by example so it can create its own recipehcltech.com.

How do machines actually "learn" from data? At the heart of it, there are a few key ingredients in any machine learning process:

- **Data:** This is the experience we give to the computer. It could be a list of house features and their prices, pictures of dogs and cats, or records of transactions. The more relevant data, the better. Quantity matters, but quality (accurate, representative data) matters too.

- **Model:** In ML, a *model* is the result of the learning process – it's the learned pattern or set of rules the computer comes up with. You can think of it as the brain of the AI for that task. Initially, the model starts blank (or with random guesses) and is refined through learning.

- **Algorithm:** The learning algorithm is the procedure or method that the computer uses to adjust the model based on the data. Different algorithms tell the computer how to find patterns. Some algorithms are simple, like finding the line of best fit through data points (regression), while others are more complex, like adjusting millions of tiny parameters in a neural network. But fundamentally, the algorithm guides the learning.

- **Training:** This is the process of feeding data into the algorithm to produce a trained model. During training, the model's performance is evaluated and improved iteratively. It's akin to a student studying with a practice set: initially making mistakes, then gradually improving by correcting those mistakes.

- **Prediction (Inference):** After training, we use the model to make predictions or decisions on new, unseen data. For example, once a spam filter model is trained on past emails, we use it to classify new incoming emails as spam or not. This stage is where the model is applied in real-world usage.

To illustrate, imagine training a simple machine learning model to recognize whether a photo contains a cat. We gather, say, 10,000 photos of pets with labels (each photo is labeled "cat" or "not cat"). During **training**, the algorithm goes through these examples and gradually tunes the model. At the start, the model might be guessing randomly. It sees a photo, guesses "cat," and then checks against the label. If it was wrong, it adjusts its internal parameters so that next time a similar image appears, it's less likely to guess the same wrong answer. If it was right, it still adjusts, but to reinforce that pattern. Over thousands of photos, the model gets better at distinguishing cat vs. not-cat by learning the common patterns (maybe it figures out that images with whiskers and pointy ears and certain shapes tend to be cats). Eventually, the model becomes accurate enough that when you give it a brand new photo it's never seen, it can confidently predict whether there's a cat in it.

One big advantage of machine learning is that models can **improve over time** as they are given more data. We aren't limited by what we initially programmed; the model can adapt. However, an ML model is only as good as its training data and algorithm. If the data is biased or limited, the model's understanding will be skewed (we'll discuss this risk more in the ethics chapter). Also, ML models don't *truly* "understand" in the way humans do – they find statistical patterns, which can sometimes lead to surprising errors if they encounter something outside their learned experience.

Machine learning isn't one single method, but rather a broad field encompassing many techniques. There are different **types of learning** for different situations, often categorized as **supervised**, **unsupervised**, or **reinforcement learning**. Don't worry about the terms right now – we will introduce each of these in its own chapter with plenty of examples. In brief: *supervised learning* is like learning with a teacher (you have labeled examples to learn from), *unsupervised learning* is like discovering patterns on your own (no given labels, the algorithm finds structure in data by itself), and *reinforcement learning* is learning by trial-and-error, receiving rewards or penalties (like training a pet with treats). These will become clearer soon.

Another term you might have heard is **deep learning**. Deep learning is essentially a particular approach to machine learning that has become very popular. It involves models called neural networks (inspired loosely by the human brain) with many layers – hence "deep." Deep learning has been a game-changer in fields like image recognition and language translation due to its ability to automatically learn complex patterns from large amounts of data. We'll dedicate a section to this concept as well, but it's basically an advanced subfield of ML.

By now, you should grasp the essence of machine learning: instead of explicitly programming a solution, we enable a machine to *learn* from examples. This concept is the cornerstone of most AI applications today. Whenever you hear about an AI that "learns" or "improves" or "predicts," it's almost certainly using machine learning under the hood. In the following chapters, we will build on this foundation, diving into the main categories of ML and other AI concepts, all explained in simple terms.

*(Summary: Machine Learning is a way to make computers learn from data rather than explicit programming ibm.com. It's like showing a computer lots of examples so it can figure out the pattern on its own – similar to how a child learns by example. Key parts of ML include data (examples), a model (the learned pattern or "brain"), and a training process where the model adjusts itself to get better using an algorithm. ML is powerful because models can improve with experience and handle complex problems that would be hard to hard-code. Next, we'll explore different types of machine learning, starting with supervised learning.)*

## Thought Exercise: Match Components

For a task like predicting sales:

1. Identify data, model, algorithm roles.

2. Match to the scenario.

3. Discuss data collection.

# Chapter 3: AI in Everyday Life – Examples and Applications

AI might sound abstract, but it's very much a part of our day-to-day world. In this chapter, we'll look at a variety of **real-world examples** of AI and ML in action. These examples will illustrate how the concepts we're discussing manifest in technology you use or encounter regularly, often making life easier or more personalized. As you go through them, you'll likely realize that you interact with AI more often than you thought!

## 3.1 Personalized Recommendations (Entertainment and Shopping)

One of the most visible uses of AI is in recommendation systems. Have you noticed how Netflix suggests movies or shows you might like, or how Amazon recommends products ("Customers who viewed this also viewed..."), or how Spotify creates a personalized playlist like "Discover Weekly" for you? These are driven by machine learning algorithms analyzing your past behaviors. The system looks at what you've watched, listened to, or bought, compares it to millions of other users' data, and finds patterns to predict what else might interest you. For example, if many users who buy item A also buy item B, the system learns this association and might recommend B to someone who bought A. Or if you've been listening to a lot of classical piano music, Spotify's AI might suggest other piano pieces or artists that fit that pattern.

These recommendation AIs use techniques ranging from simple statistics to complex ML models. A common approach is called **collaborative filtering**, where the AI finds people with similar tastes and recommends to you something that those similar users liked. Another approach is **content-based**, where the AI looks at attributes of the items (genre of a movie, tempo of a song) and recommends items with similar attributes to what you liked. Often, modern systems combine multiple methods for better accuracy.

From a user's perspective, the result is that the service feels *tailored* to you. Netflix's front page is different for each person, and even the cover images might be chosen by AI to appeal to your tastes (for instance, highlighting the action scenes for an action fan). The goal is to help you discover things you'll enjoy without you having to search manually through huge catalogs. It's a win-win: you get relevant suggestions, and the service keeps you engaged. Just keep in mind,

these are predictions based on data –
they might occasionally miss the mark,
especially if your tastes change or if
you're interested in something outside
your usual pattern.

## 3.2 Virtual Assistants and Smart Speakers

Virtual assistants like **Siri**, **Google Assistant**, **Alexa**, or **Cortana** are commonplace now, either on our phones or as smart speakers in our homes. These assistants use AI to understand natural language commands and respond usefully. For example, if you ask Siri, "Remind me to call Mom at 7 PM," Siri uses **Natural Language Processing (NLP)** (a branch of AI) to interpret your speech, identify the task (a reminder) and the details (who to call, when), and then schedule that reminder in your phone. If you ask Alexa, "What's the weather tomorrow?", it converts your voice to text, figures out you want a weather report for tomorrow, fetches that information, and then uses a text-to-speech system to read it out in a friendly voice.

These tasks involve multiple AI components working together: voice **speech recognition** to convert the sound waves of your voice into words (AI models are trained to recognize spoken words – imagine learning from thousands of hours of recorded speech), language understanding to interpret the meaning of the sentence, and sometimes dialogue management to carry multi-step conversations. The assistant also continually learns to improve its understanding of your voice and preferences. For instance, Alexa might learn your music taste if you frequently ask it to play songs, and then it could personalize radio station suggestions.

AI also helps these assistants perform tasks autonomously. If you say "Book me an Uber to the airport," an AI behind the scenes processes that, interacts with the Uber API, and completes the task, almost like a virtual concierge. The more you use these assistants, the more data they gather to refine their models (for example, adapting to your accent or figuring out your home and work locations for contextual answers). Modern smart assistants even exhibit a degree of AI *agent* behavior – they perceive input (your voice), decide on an action (which service to invoke or what answer to give), and produce an output (speech or an action), aligning with the agent concepts we will cover later.

A quick everyday example: When driving, you might use voice commands to stay hands-free. You say, *"Hey Google, send a text to John: I'm running late."* The AI has to parse that, understand the contact name and message, and send it via your messaging app. This string of operations happens in a few seconds, powered by AI models that have been trained on huge datasets of language. The ease of doing this now belies the complexity under the hood.

## 3.3 Image Recognition and Vision Applications

AI's ability to interpret images has improved dramatically, thanks largely to deep learning. A common example is the **face recognition** feature on smartphones. When you use your face to unlock the phone, an AI algorithm is checking if the face matches the owner's face. The phone's camera captures an image, and an AI model (often a deep neural network) has been trained to recognize the unique features of your face (perhaps the distances between your eyes, the shape of your jaw, etc.). It compares the live image to the stored model of your face. If it's a close match, voila – unlocked. This is done securely and locally on the device. The model was "trained" on many images of you (often during setup it asks you to look from different angles) and also relies on having been pre-trained on large datasets of faces to know how to pick out distinguishing features iotforall.com.

Beyond personal device use, face recognition is used in other contexts – e.g., tagging friends on Facebook (the app suggests who is in a photo by recognizing their faces), or security cameras that can identify known individuals. This raises some privacy concerns we'll discuss later, but technically, it showcases AI's proficiency in pattern recognition.

Another cool example: **visual filters** (like on Snapchat or Instagram). When you use a filter that gives you dog ears or changes your gender appearance, AI vision models are identifying key points on your face (eyes, nose, etc.) and then overlaying graphics that move with you. That face detection and landmark recognition is powered by trained ML models.

**Object recognition** in general is widely used. Google Photos can organize your pictures by recognizing objects or scenes (e.g., find all photos with "beach" or "wedding" or even a specific person). Self-driving cars use multiple cameras and AI vision to identify lane markings, other cars, pedestrians, traffic signs and lights – essentially giving the car a visual understanding of its surroundings. In retail, stores are experimenting with AI cameras that can recognize products you pick up (as in Amazon's prototype grocery stores with automated checkout).

One more everyday use: **scanning documents**. Apps that scan paper documents use AI to not only capture the image but often to do OCR (Optical Character Recognition) – turning a photo of text into actual digital text. That involves an AI reading the shapes of letters. If you've ever deposited a check via a banking app and it read the amount, that's AI at work.

## 3.4 Email Spam Filtering and Smart Replies

Email providers heavily leverage AI to make your inbox manageable. The spam filter we mentioned earlier is a classic **supervised learning** application. Over years, these filters have been trained on millions of emails that were marked as spam or not spamv7labs.com. The model learns the subtle cues that distinguish unsolicited junk mail from legitimate mail. Some cues are obvious (certain keywords or sender addresses), but others might be statistical patterns that aren't obvious to humans. The result is that modern spam filters catch the vast majority of spam, and only rarely misclassify a legitimate email (though it does happen occasionally – that's why it's good to glance at your spam folder).

Beyond spam, email services now also use AI for things like **smart replies** and **email categorization**. If you use Gmail, you've probably seen the three suggested quick reply buttons at the bottom of an email (like "Sure, sounds good!" or "I'll get back to you."). That's generated by an AI model that has been trained on tons of email data to predict likely replies. Similarly, the "Promotions" or "Updates" tabs in Gmail are sorted by an AI that classifies incoming mail into categories like Promotions, Social, Updates, etc., to help organize your inbox.

Another neat feature is **typing autocompletion** (e.g., Gmail's Smart Compose). As you type an email, it might gray out a suggestion to finish your sentence. This uses a predictive language model (a kind of AI model) to guess what you're going to say based on context. For example, if you type "I'll reach out to you next", it might suggest "week" as the next word. These models learn from analyzing a vast number of sentences and emails to understand common patterns of phrasing. Essentially, the AI tries to save you keystrokes by completing common expressions.

### 3.5 Social Media Feeds and Content Moderation

If you use social media platforms like Facebook, Instagram, Twitter, or LinkedIn, AI is extensively at play. Your **news feed** on these platforms is personalized by AI algorithms. Since there are far more posts from friends, pages, and accounts than anyone can read, an algorithm decides which ones to show you first. How does it decide? By predicting what content is most relevant or engaging to you. It looks at your past interactions – whose posts you liked or commented on, what topics seem to interest you, which posts are currently popular overall – and then ranks new posts in an order it believes you'll find compelling. This is why no two people see the same Facebook feed even if they have similar friends.

AI also helps **moderate content** on social mediaiotforall.com. With billions of posts, it's impossible for human moderators to review everything. Machine learning models scan content to detect things like hate speech, explicit imagery, or disinformation. For instance, AI might flag a post containing certain slurs or known extremist symbols for review, or automatically remove images that match a database of inappropriate content. On platforms like YouTube, AI is used to identify and remove videos that violate policies, though it's not perfect and often a human review is needed for borderline cases. The goal is to keep these platforms safe and in line with community standards at scale, and AI provides the first line of defense.

Social media also uses AI for **face tagging** (as mentioned, recognizing your friends in a photo), **language translation** (automatically translating foreign language posts), and even **augmented reality** effects (like Instagram filters similar to Snapchat's). And from a business perspective, AIs power the **ad targeting** – based on your behavior, the platform's algorithms decide which ads you might be most likely to respond to, thereby serving different ads to different users.

## 3.6 Healthcare and Diagnostics

AI is making significant inroads in healthcare, assisting doctors and medical staff in various ways. One prominent application is in **medical image analysis**. Doctors often have to examine images like X-rays, MRI scans, or CT scans for signs of disease (tumors, fractures, etc.). AI models, especially deep learning models, have shown remarkable ability in identifying patterns in these images. In some cases, AI systems can detect certain conditions as well as or even better than human specialists bmcmededuc.biomedcentral.com. For example, researchers have developed AI that can examine mammograms (breast X-rays) and spot early signs of breast cancer. In one study, an AI system correctly identified 90% of cancer cases in the data, whereas human radiologists identified about

78% – showing that the AI, with its tireless pattern recognition, can provide a helpful second opinion or catch things a human might miss bmcmededuc.biomedcentral.com. That doesn't mean AI replaces the doctor; rather, it acts as a diagnostic aid, highlighting areas of concern so the doctor can make a more informed decision.

Another example is AI in **ophthalmology**: there are AI tools that analyze retinal scans to detect conditions like diabetic retinopathy (an eye disease from diabetes) early on. Similarly, AI is used to analyze skin lesion images for skin cancer, or to read pathology slides (tissue samples) for signs of disease.

Beyond imaging, AI helps in predicting patient outcomes or hospital resource needs. For instance, hospitals use AI to predict which patients are at higher risk of complications or readmission, allowing for preventative care. AI can also assist in **drug discovery** by analyzing large datasets of chemical compounds and biological effects to suggest new drug candidates – though that's more behind-the-scenes in pharma companies than in everyday patient interaction.

If you've interacted with **chatbot symptom checkers** (like apps or websites where you input symptoms and it suggests possible conditions or advice), that's another use of AI. These services use large medical datasets and probabilities to guide you on whether you might just need rest or should see a doctor, etc.

Lastly, administrative tasks in healthcare, like transcribing doctors' notes or scheduling, are also being streamlined by AI (for example, speech recognition to transcribe a doctor's dictated notes directly into medical records, saving time).

## 3.7 Finance: Fraud Detection and Personal Banking

The finance industry has embraced AI for a variety of purposes. A very important one is **fraud detection**. Whenever you swipe your credit card or do an online transaction, AI systems in the background are monitoring for unusual patterns that might indicate fraud. For example, if your card is suddenly used in a different country or for an unusually large purchase that doesn't fit your spending history, an AI might flag it. These models are trained on historical transaction data, including known fraudulent transactions, to recognize the signs of fraudiotforall.com. The system might automatically decline a transaction that looks highly suspicious or send you an alert to confirm if it was really you. Banks also use AI to detect suspicious patterns in bank accounts (like money laundering activities) by analyzing sequences of transactions.

AI is also providing **personalized finance advice and automation**. Many banking apps now have virtual assistants or analytics that will, for instance, categorize your spending (how much you spent on food vs. travel this month) and even alert you if you're spending more than usual. Some apps use AI to predict your cash flow – e.g., warning you that you might overdraft based on upcoming bills and past income patterns. Robo-advisors in investment (like Betterment or Robinhood's suggestions) use algorithms to help tailor investment portfolios to individuals' goals and risk tolerance.

In stock trading, AI algorithms (quantitative trading models) comb through market data at high speed to make trading decisions – though that's more for professionals and behind the scenes. If you use any automated investing or even something like an AI-powered loan approval system (where the bank's model assesses your risk beyond just a credit score), that's AI in action.

Finally, **customer service chatbots** for banks and credit card companies have become common. Instead of waiting on hold, you might chat with an AI chatbot on the bank's website to get information like your account balance, recent transactions, or help with common issues. The chatbot uses NLP to understand your questions and provide answers, escalating to a human agent if it gets confused or if the question is too complex.

## 3.8 Smart Homes and IoT Devices

Our homes are getting smarter with AI embedded in various gadgets. A prime example is the **smart thermostat** (like Google Nest). A Nest thermostat uses machine learning to learn your schedule and temperature preferences. In the first couple of weeks, you might manually adjust the temperature (cooler at night, off when you're at work, warmer in the evening, etc.). The thermostat observes these adjustments and starts to detect a pattern. After a while, it begins to automatically schedule temperature changes to match what it thinks you typically do. It's essentially learning from your behavior (and also using sensors to detect if you're home or not). Over time, it optimizes to both keep you comfortable and save energy by not running heating/cooling when not needed. This is a form of AI *agent* in a way – it perceives (time of day, whether you're home, current temperature), decides (should I turn heating on or off now?), and acts (controls the furnace/AC).

**Smart security cameras** for home use AI for motion detection and even recognition. Cameras like the Ring or Google Nest Cam can differentiate between a person vs. an animal vs. just tree branches moving. Some systems even attempt facial recognition to tell you "Family member vs. Stranger" alerts. This is done by on-device or cloud-based neural networks analyzing the video feed in real time.

Robot vacuum cleaners (like Roomba) are another household AI agent. Early robot vacuums were fairly dumb – bumping randomly. Newer models create a map of your house, know where obstacles are, and systematically clean. They use sensors (bump sensors, cameras or LIDAR) and AI algorithms to map rooms and plan optimal paths. They also learn where high dirt areas are (maybe your kitchen) and can focus there. Some even integrate with smart assistants (you can say "Alexa, tell Roomba to clean under the dining table" and it will target that area if it has the map knowledge).

**Voice-controlled devices** beyond assistants also count – for instance, smart TVs with voice search (using AI to parse your speech for show titles or genres) or smart fridges that might keep an inventory and suggest recipes (using some image recognition to see what's inside, perhaps).

### 3.9 Navigation and Travel

Gone are the days of printed maps; most of us rely on GPS navigation apps like Google Maps or Waze, which heavily employ AI. **Navigation apps** not only show you a map, but they intelligently find the best route and update it based on real-time conditions. These apps predict traffic by analyzing current data and historical patterns – for example, they know that on weekdays at 5pm a certain highway gets congested. If there's an accident, AI processes the speed data of phones/cars on the road and quickly infers a slowdown, suggesting alternate routes. They even estimate your arrival time taking into account likely traffic at different segments of your journey (which is why they're usually pretty accurate unless something truly unpredictable occurs).

Waze takes it further by crowdsourcing reports (incidents, police, etc.) and using that data in real-time route updates – the app's algorithms weigh the delays and reroute users accordingly. The capability for quick decision-making here (should you detour or stick to current route given a small delay vs. distance trade-off) comes from AI optimization algorithms.

**Ridesharing apps** (Uber, Lyft) also use AI for matching drivers to riders, setting dynamic prices, and routing drivers. For example, when you request a ride, an AI algorithm determines which nearby driver should get the request (to minimize wait and drive time). They also predict areas of high demand and may proactive position drivers. The pricing (surge pricing) is algorithmic based on supply and demand, which is a simpler form of automated decision-making.

## 3.10 Other Industry Examples

To give a broader taste:

- **Manufacturing:** AI-powered robots and machines on factory floors perform tasks like quality inspection using computer vision (identifying defective products by looking at them) and predictive maintenance (sensing when a machine is likely to fail soon and alerting staff to fix it proactively).

- **Agriculture:** Farmers use AI for precision farming – e.g., drones with AI vision survey fields to detect crop health, or smart irrigation systems use ML to optimize water use based on weather forecasts and soil data.

- **Education:** AI tutors or learning platforms (like Duolingo for language learning) adapt to the student's level. If the student struggles with a concept, the AI can present more practice for that concept. Some universities use AI to proctor exams (monitor video for cheating) or to help identify students who might be at risk of failing by analyzing their engagement data.

- **Customer Service:** Beyond chatbots, even email inquiry sorting and support ticket routing is done by AI. If you email a company, an AI might read it and decide which department or agent is best suited to handle it based on the content.

- **Art and Creativity:** There are AI tools that generate art, music, or writing. For instance, AI can help photographers by automatically enhancing photos or even composing shots (some smart cameras have AI scene detection that adjusts settings based on whether it sees a landscape, a person, night time, etc.). In marketing, AI can generate product descriptions or social media posts draft for humans to fine-tune.

As you can see, AI is a versatile technology finding use in many domains. Often it works quietly in the background to make systems smarter and more efficient. Importantly, each of these applications ties back to the fundamental concepts of AI we are discussing. Whether it's a supervised learning model labeling an image, an unsupervised model clustering user tastes, or an AI agent deciding an action (like a robot vacuum's next move), the same core ideas apply. In the next chapters, we'll dive into those core ideas – starting with the different ways machine learning occurs. As you read on, think back to these examples; you'll start to connect how an AI choosing a move in chess isn't fundamentally different from an AI suggesting a song – both are making decisions based on learned patterns, just in different contexts.

### Case Study: Duolingo's Adaptive Learning

Duolingo's AI tailors exercises, improving retention by 20%.

### Thought Exercise: AI in Apps

1. List app features using AI.

2. Hypothesize tasks.

3. Verify online.

*(Summary: AI is already widely used in daily life. We see it in personalized recommendations on Netflix and Amazon, in smart assistants like Siri and Alexa that understand our voice, in image recognition for tagging photos or unlocking phones[iotforall.com](iotforall.com), and in social media feeds tailored by AI [iotforall.com](iotforall.com). It's helping doctors diagnose diseases from scans and banking systems detect fraud. Even our home appliances like thermostats and robot vacuums use AI to learn and adapt. These real-world applications are powered by the AI and ML concepts we are learning – they demonstrate how useful those concepts are in practice. Next, we will explore how AI learns to do these tasks by looking at different types of machine learning.)*

# Chapter 4: Supervised Learning – Learning with a Teacher

Now that we've seen what AI can do, let's dig into how we actually *train* an AI to perform such tasks. The first, and most common, approach is **Supervised Learning**. This is the type of machine learning that drives many of the examples we discussed (spam filtering, image recognition, predictive text, etc.). Supervised learning is akin to learning under the guidance of a teacher or from an answer key. The idea is straightforward: we provide the algorithm with example inputs and the desired outputs (the "correct answers") during training, so it can learn the relationship between them ibm.com.

Imagine you're trying to teach a child to differentiate between apples and oranges. One way is to give the child a bunch of fruits one by one, and each time say "This is an apple" or "This is an orange." After enough examples, the child starts to learn the visual differences. In machine learning terms, the photos of fruits are the **input**, and the labels "apple" or "orange" are the **output**. The child's brain adjusts its internal model with each example (maybe noticing color and shape as clues). Eventually, when shown a new fruit, the child can correctly say whether it's an apple or an orange. That's supervised learning in a nutshell: learning from labeled examples.

Formally, in supervised learning we have a **training dataset** composed of input-output pairs. Each pair consists of the features (the input data describing a thing) and a label (the correct output for that thing). The goal is for the algorithm to learn a general rule or mapping from inputs to outputs, so that it can predict the output for new inputs that it hasn't seen before.

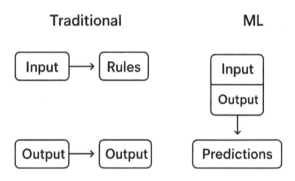

Let's break that down with a concrete example: **email spam filtering**, which we've mentioned. Here:

- **Input**: The content of an email (perhaps represented by various features like presence of certain words, sender address, etc.).

- **Output label**: "Spam" or "Not Spam" (sometimes called "ham" for not spam). We train a supervised learning model by feeding it lots of emails that people have already labeled as spam or not. One email might have the label spam, another not spam, and so on. The learning algorithm looks at an email's features and the given label, and tries to adjust an internal model to be able to predict that label from those features. If the model's current state incorrectly predicts the label, the algorithm tweaks the model to reduce the erroribm.com. If it's correct, it can reinforce that. Over *many* emails, the model parameters get tuned such that it can accurately classify the training examples. Then we hope it generalizes to new emails — meaning the patterns it learned are generally true of spam vs non-spam.

Common applications of supervised learning include classification (assigning categories, like spam vs not spam, or diagnosing a patient as disease vs no disease) and regression (predicting a continuous value, like tomorrow's temperature or a house price based on features). For instance, a house price prediction model might take features of a house (size, location, number of bedrooms) as input and output a predicted price. It would be trained on historical data of house features along with their sold prices as labels. Likewise, an image recognition model might be trained on thousands of images labeled with the object they contain (cat, dog, etc.), so it learns to classify images into categories.

To solidify understanding, here's a simple **pseudocode** example of how supervised training works in principle:

vbnet

CopyEdit

```
# Pseudocode: Training a Supervised Learning Model (e.g., Spam Filter)


initialize model (start with random weights or no knowledge)
for each labeled example in the training dataset:
    input_data = example.data     # e.g., the email content
    true_label = example.label    # e.g., "Spam" or "Not Spam"
```

```
# Step 1: model makes a prediction
based on current knowledge

predicted_label =
model.predict(input_data)


# Step 2: compare prediction to the
true label to calculate error

error = loss(predicted_label,
true_label)


# Step 3: adjust the model to reduce
error

model.update_parameters(error,
input_data, true_label)


end for
```

# After many iterations, the model has learned from its mistakes.

# It should now predict correctly (or with much less error) on similar data.

In simpler terms:

1.  The model takes a guess for each example.

2.  We tell it how wrong or right that guess was (since we have the answer).

3.  The model then **learns** by tweaking itself to do better next time on that example.

4.  Repeat this thousands or millions of times.

Eventually, the model's guesses get pretty good, not just for the examples it saw, but hopefully for new examples too. This is analogous to a student doing practice problems with an answer key – checking each answer and learning from mistakes.

It's worth noting that supervised learning typically requires a lot of **labeled data**. Getting high-quality labeled data can sometimes be a challenge (someone has to provide those correct answers). In many industries, preparing the training data (also called **data labeling or annotation**) is a major part of deploying AI. For example, to train a self-driving car's vision system, humans had to label millions of images or videos to indicate, "this region is a pedestrian", "this is a lane line", etc., so the model could learn to recognize those. Similarly, medical AI models are trained on datasets where doctors have marked the images or cases with the correct diagnosis.

Supervised learning works very well when you can clearly define the problem and gather examples of correct outputs. It's like learning by example at scale. However, there are situations where you might not have labels readily available or where the task is more exploratory – that's where other forms of learning come in (like unsupervised). But before moving on, let's consider a few more details and examples in supervised learning:

- **Example: Predicting House Prices.** Suppose you want an AI to estimate house prices. You collect a dataset of 10,000 houses, each with features like square footage, number of bedrooms, zip code, lot size, etc., and each with the actual sale price (the label). You choose a supervised learning algorithm, say linear regression or a neural network. During training, for each house, the model predicts a price and compares it to the actual price. If a house was sold for $500k but the model predicted $400k, it has an error of $100k for that example. The algorithm then adjusts, maybe increasing weights on certain features that might increase the predicted price (like zip code if that area is pricier). After many houses, the model might learn, for instance, how each feature generally contributes to price. The end result is a model that, given a new house's features, can output a reasonable predicted price close to what it might actually sell for. Real estate websites use such models to give those "Zestimate" or price estimate for properties.

- **Example: Image Classification (Cats vs. Dogs).** You have 1,000 cat photos and 1,000 dog photos. You label them accordingly. You choose a deep learning model (a neural network) because images are complex. Training starts: the model might initially just guess randomly. For each photo, it outputs something like "I think there's a 0.7 probability this is a dog" – basically a score – and that is compared to the true label (say the photo is actually a cat, which we can represent as 0 for dog and 1 for cat in a numeric way or vice versa). The difference is measured (that's the error). The neural network then adjusts its internal connections (weights) slightly in a direction that would make it more likely to say "cat" next time for that image. This involves some math (backpropagation, gradient descent) that we don't need to detail here, but conceptually it's "tune the knobs to reduce error." After many iterations, the model might accurately distinguish cats and dogs – it has essentially discovered what features in the image (fur patterns, ear shapes, etc.) differentiate them, without us explicitly coding those features. We just provided many examples and corrections.

Supervised learning algorithms come in many flavors: linear models, decision trees, random forests, support vector machines, neural networks, etc. Each has its own way of representing the model and learning from data, but they all share the common theme of needing labeled examples. The choice of algorithm can depend on the problem size, the amount of data, and whether the relationship is simple or very complex. For instance, linear regression might suffice for a simple relationship, whereas a neural network might handle something like image recognition which is highly complex.

One thing to be careful about is **overfitting** – when a model becomes too tailored to the training data and doesn't generalize well to new data. It's like a student who memorized the practice problems and answers but didn't grasp the underlying concept – they might fail the test if the questions are slightly different. In ML, if you have a very powerful model and relatively small data, it might end up just memorizing each training example. Techniques like having more data, simplifying the model, or using validation checks help ensure the model actually *learns* the pattern rather than memorizing. But that's a bit beyond our current scope. Just be aware that more complex isn't always better – the model needs to strike a balance, a concept called **generalization**.

To summarize supervised learning: it's teaching by example with feedback. It has been hugely successful and underpins a lot of AI services. Whenever you see an AI making predictions (like whether something is X or Y, or predicting a value), and you know there was historical data with answers, supervised learning was likely used. In the next section, we'll switch perspective to scenarios where such labeled answers aren't available, and how AI can still learn from data on its own.

(Summary: Supervised learning is when an AI is trained on examples that each come with a correct answer, much like a student learning with a teacher or answer key*ibm.com*. The AI model makes predictions on training examples and is corrected using the known answers, gradually learning the right patterns. This method is widely used for tasks like classifying emails as spam/not spam, recognizing objects in images, or predicting numbers (like house prices)*v7labs.com*. It requires lots of labeled data but can achieve high accuracy. We feed the algorithm input-output pairs, and it learns a mapping so it can predict outputs for new inputs. In pseudocode, it's essentially: for each example, compare prediction to truth and adjust. Supervised learning is powerful *when correct output labels are available, but what about cases where they aren't? That brings us to unsupervised learning.)*

# Chapter 5: Unsupervised Learning – Finding Hidden Patterns

Not all learning happens with a teacher. Sometimes, we just have a lot of data with no explicit labels or correct answers, and we want the AI to make sense of it. This is where **Unsupervised Learning** comes into play. In unsupervised learning, the algorithm is given data and left to discover patterns, structures, or relationships within that data **without any labeled answers**. It's like being handed a stack of puzzle pieces without the picture on the box – you have to figure out how they might fit together using only the pieces themselves.

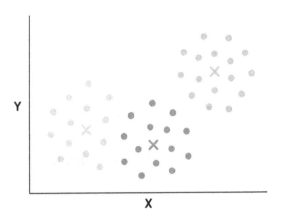

An everyday analogy: imagine you have a collection of miscellaneous coins from around the world mixed together, and you've never seen these currencies before. No one tells you which coin is from which country. If you sort them, you might naturally group them by similarities – perhaps by size, color, and design. You might end up with clusters of coins that look similar. Maybe you figure out, "These shiny goldish small ones form one group, those larger silver ones with ridges form another." Essentially, you clustered the coins by appearance. Later you might learn the names (labels) of each currency and realize you had grouped all Euro cents in one pile, all Japanese yen coins in another, etc. What you did initially was unsupervised learning – finding structure (groups) without labels.

Unsupervised learning often involves **clustering** and **association**:

- **Clustering**: the algorithm divides the data into groups (clusters) such that items in the same cluster are more similar to each other than to those in other clusters. It's about grouping similar things.

- **Association (or Association Rule Learning)**: the algorithm finds rules that describe relationships between variables in the data. A classic example is market basket analysis: finding that "people who buy bread and butter often also buy jam" – an association rule.

Let's talk about clustering first, as it's the most intuitive unsupervised task. Suppose you run a business and you have a large customer dataset with various attributes (age, buying habits, interests, etc.) but you don't have any predefined segment labels. You might use a clustering algorithm to discover **customer segments**. The algorithm might tell you, for example, that your customers naturally fall into three groups: one group is, say, young urban professionals who buy premium products; another is budget-conscious families; a third is older retirees who buy specific items. These groupings were not given to the algorithm explicitly – it discovered them from purchasing patterns and demographics. This can inform marketing strategies (tailoring different approaches to each segment) even though you didn't start with those labels.

Another example: **grouping news articles**. If you feed a bunch of news articles into an unsupervised algorithm, it might cluster them into topics. Maybe one cluster corresponds to sports articles, another to political news, another to tech, etc., purely based on the words that appear in the articles (even without any labels like "sports" attached). The algorithm might identify that certain words like "game, score, team, season" tend to occur together, indicating a sports cluster, whereas words like "government, election, policy" cluster a different set.

A practical everyday use of clustering is in **photo management**. Some photo apps use AI to group photos by faces (even if you haven't named the people yet). The app's algorithm can process all your photos and cluster them by the similarity of faces – effectively finding out how many distinct people appear in your photo collection and grouping photos by each person. Later, you might label cluster #7 as "Alice" once you see all of Alice's pictures grouped. The initial grouping of faces was unsupervised.

Unsupervised learning is also at the heart of **recommendation engines** in a certain sense. Earlier we explained how recommendations can be seen through supervised or simple association, but one approach is to use clustering: cluster users based on behavior and then recommend what similar users liked (this is one way collaborative filtering can be implemented). Another unsupervised element in recommendations is **dimensionality reduction** (e.g., an algorithm like PCA – principal component analysis) which reduces complex preference data into a simpler form to match users to content.

Another key unsupervised task: **anomaly detection**. Here, rather than clusters, the goal is to find data points that don't fit any strong pattern – the "odd ones out". For example, a bank might use anomaly detection on transactions: without knowing what is fraud (no label), the algorithm might flag transactions that are very different from normal activity. Perhaps one transaction is far larger than what that user usually does, at an odd time, from a new location – the algorithm sees it as not fitting the "cluster" of that user's usual behavior, thus an anomaly. This can then be investigated further. Essentially, the model has learned what "normal" looks like in an unsupervised way, and then anything not normal is suspicious.

To understand unsupervised learning more concretely, consider the popular algorithm **k-means clustering** (don't worry about the name too much, but it's widely used). The idea is:

- You tell the algorithm roughly how many clusters you think are in the data (say k = 3 clusters).

- The algorithm initially picks 3 random points as cluster centers.

- Then it goes through the data points and assigns each data point to the nearest cluster center.

- Next, it recalculates the cluster centers as the mean (average) of all points assigned to each cluster.

- It repeats the assign-and-update process until things stabilize (points aren't switching clusters much). In the end, you have 3 clusters and the center of each cluster (hence k "means"). You might then interpret what those clusters represent by looking at the characteristics of points in them.

For example, imagine we have height and weight data of a group of animals (without labels of species). If we apply clustering with k=2, perhaps the algorithm will separate them into two clusters – one cluster could be heavy, tall animals (maybe those turn out to be horses) and another cluster of lighter, shorter animals (maybe those are dogs). We didn't tell it "dog" or "horse"; it just grouped by the numeric similarity, which happened to correspond to species.

One challenging aspect of unsupervised learning is that it's not always obvious **what the right answer is**. With supervised learning, we have ground truth labels to measure accuracy against. With unsupervised, we might not have a clear metric of success because we are exploring unknown structure. It often requires human interpretation. For instance, a clustering algorithm might output some clusters, but a human analyst has to make sense of them and decide if they are useful or meaningful. It's a bit of an art to validate unsupervised results – you may use domain knowledge or external evaluations.

However, unsupervised learning is incredibly useful because in the real world, *unlabeled data is far more abundant than labeled data*. Think of all the data being generated – logs, texts, images – only a small fraction is neatly labeled. Unsupervised methods help us tap into that wealth of raw data to see patterns. Sometimes, unsupervised learning is a preliminary step to guide further analysis. For example, clustering might be used to pre-segment data before applying supervised learning within each segment, or to identify outliers to focus on.

One famous unsupervised learning story: Google's DeepMind researchers once let a neural network just watch a bunch of YouTube videos without telling it anything. It was a form of unsupervised learning (technically a type of deep learning called autoencoder). The interesting result was that one of the things the model learned to detect by itself was cats! (Apparently, cats are common enough and have distinctive enough features in YouTube videos that the neural net formed a "cat" neuron internally.) This wasn't because it was told "find cats," it just recognized a frequently occurring pattern. This anecdote shows how unsupervised learning can surface notable patterns in data automaticallyibm.com (in this case, the pattern of "catness" in images).

Another area of unsupervised learning is **feature extraction**. Sometimes unsupervised techniques are used to preprocess data, to find the most informative features. For instance, in text analysis, an unsupervised model might learn topics from a set of documents, and those topics (essentially clusters of words) can then be used as features for a supervised task like categorizing documents. This blends into a bit more technical territory, but it highlights that unsupervised and supervised can be combined in pipelines.

To summarize unsupervised learning:

- There are no given labels or answers; the algorithm tries to **make sense of the data on its own**.

- It's great for exploring data, finding groupings, patterns, trends, or anomalies.

- The results often need interpretation; the "correctness" is sometimes subjective or application-dependent.

- It's used in customer segmentation, recommendation, anomaly detection, topic modeling, data compression, and more.

- It leverages unstructured and unlabeled data, which makes it very powerful in the era of big data.

*(Summary: Unsupervised learning deals with data that has no labels or predefined correct answers. The AI tries to find patterns or groupings on its own. A common example is clustering – grouping similar data points together (like grouping customers by buying patterns or grouping images by visual similarity)v7labs.com. Unlike supervised learning, there's no explicit "right or wrong" during training; the algorithm is discovering structure. This is useful for tasks like discovering customer segments, detecting unusual events (anomaly detection), or organizing information (like grouping*

*news by topic) without needing someone to hand-label everything. Unsupervised learning helps us make sense of large volumes of raw data. Next, we'll explore a different approach: an AI learning by trial and error through feedback, known as reinforcement learning.)*

# Chapter 6: Reinforcement Learning – Learning by Trial and Error

We've covered learning from examples with answers (supervised) and learning by finding patterns without answers (unsupervised). Now we turn to a very different paradigm: **Reinforcement Learning (RL)**. Reinforcement learning is inspired by how beings learn through experience — by interacting with their environment, making mistakes, and gradually improving. It's often compared to how you might train a pet or how a child learns to perform a new skill by trial and error. In reinforcement learning, an **agent** learns what actions to take in an environment in order to maximize some notion of cumulative reward.

A classic analogy is **training a dog** to do a trick. Imagine you're training a dog to fetch a ball. You can't directly tell the dog what to do (no supervised labels like "move 5 feet forward, turn left, grab ball"); instead, the dog tries various things. When it does something right, like taking a step toward the ball, you say "Good!" and maybe give it a treat (reward). If it does something wrong, like run in the wrong direction, you might say "No" or give no reward. Over time, the dog learns that certain behaviors lead to treats and others don't, and it starts favoring the actions that get rewards. **This is reinforcement learning** in a nutshell: the dog is the agent, it's exploring actions, and feedback comes in the form of rewards (treats) or lack thereof unaligned.io.

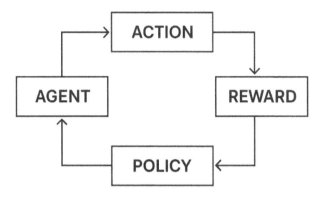

In the AI context, think of an agent as a software program (or a robot) placed in an environment. The environment could be anything: a chess board, a video game, a physical world simulation, a data center cooling system, etc. The agent can take certain **actions** in that environment (move a pawn, press left/right in the game, adjust a thermostat). For each action, it receives some **feedback** in the form of a **reward** (a numerical value). The goal of the agent is to learn a policy (a strategy) for choosing actions that maximizes the total reward it accumulates over time[unaligned.io](https://unaligned.io).

Unlike supervised learning, in RL there is not always an immediate correct answer for each step. Instead of labeled output, we have rewards that might be delayed. For example, if an agent is playing a maze game, it might wander for a while with no reward until it finally finds the exit and gets a big reward. That one reward at the end needs to reinforce all the right actions that led to it. The agent has to credit which actions were important for that success (or failure). This credit assignment problem is part of what makes RL challenging.

Let's outline the key components in reinforcement learning:

- **Agent**: The learner or decision-maker (e.g., a computer program controlling a character in a game).

- **Environment**: Everything the agent interacts with (the game, the world, or the simulated scenario).

- **State**: A snapshot of the environment at a given time – the information the agent has to decide on an action. For instance, the state could be the positions of all pieces on a chess board, or the current location and velocity of a robot, or the last screen of a video game.

- **Actions**: The set of moves the agent can make. In chess, the actions are the legal moves of pieces. In a robot, actions could be turning wheels or moving arms. The agent's job is to choose an action at each step.

- **Reward**: A feedback signal from the environment. It's a number that tells the agent what it did was good or bad in terms of achieving the goal. The agent's objective is to maximize the cumulative reward (often called return). The reward can be positive (like a treat, or points in a game) or negative (punishment, or point loss), or zero (neutral).

- **Policy**: The strategy that the agent uses to decide actions based on the state. The policy can be simple (a table mapping states to actions) or complex (a neural network taking state as input and outputting an action choice probability). The policy is what we want to learn/improve.

- **Episode**: Many RL tasks are divided into episodes (like one play of a game from start to finish). At the end of an episode (like game over or task completed), the agent's accumulated reward is evaluated, and then it might start a new episode, learning from previous ones.

Here's how a typical reinforcement learning loop works, step by step:

1. The agent observes the current **state** of the environment.

2. Based on its current policy (which might be initially random), the agent chooses an **action**.

3. The environment receives the action and transitions to a new state. The agent receives a

**reward** associated with that action (could be immediate or maybe zero until something notable happens).

4. The agent now observes the new state and the reward. It updates its policy based on the outcome – if the reward was good, it will try to make actions that lead to similar outcomes more likely in the future; if the reward was bad (or there was a penalty), it will learn to avoid the actions that led there unaligned.io.

5. Repeat this cycle continuously or until an episode ends. If the episode ends (goal reached or failure or time limit), possibly give a final reward (like winning a game might give +1, losing -1, tie 0, for example), then reset to a

new episode and continue learning.

Over many, many iterations, the agent's policy should get better at choosing actions that yield higher rewards. This is analogous to a child learning to ride a bicycle: at first they wobble and fall (negative reward, ouch), but with practice they figure out how to balance and steer (leading to smoother rides, positive intrinsic reward or praise).

Let's put this into a more concrete scenario: **a simple game**. Consider the classic game of *Pac-Man*. Pac-Man (the agent) moves around a maze eating pellets (small reward for each pellet), trying to clear the level, while avoiding ghosts (getting caught by a ghost is a big negative reward because it loses a life). There are also power pellets that allow Pac-Man to eat ghosts for a short time (eating a ghost gives a high reward). How would an RL approach this? Initially, Pac-Man's AI might move randomly, often dying quickly. But occasionally, random moves result in eating a pellet (small positive feedback). The algorithm (e.g., Q-learning or a policy gradient method – different RL algorithms) updates the policy so that moves that tend to lead to pellets (and not to immediate death) are more favored. It might still die a lot, but over many games, it learns paths that pick up pellets. Maybe by chance it eats a power pellet and then a ghost, getting a big reward; the policy update will strongly reinforce the sequence of actions that led to that. Over time, the agent becomes adept at clearing levels: it has learned a strategy (like go for power pellets, chase ghosts when powered up, run away when not, systematically clear pellets) all through trial and error, guided by the points (rewards) it received.

A real-world example of reinforcement learning: **AlphaGo**, the AI that mastered the board game Go. AlphaGo learned by reinforcement learning (combined with some supervised learning to get started). It played millions of games against itself, each time adjusting its strategy to maximize its win ratetheguardian.com. Wins gave positive reward, losses negative (or zero for draw scenarios). Through this self-play, it discovered strategies and moves that humans had never considered, eventually beating the world championtheguardian.com. In essence, it learned by playing (trial and error), improving as it went – classic RL.

Another example: **robotics**. Consider a robotic arm learning to pick up an object. We can program it via reinforcement: give a positive reward when it successfully grasps the object, and perhaps a small negative reward for failed attempts (or time wasted). The robot tries different angles and grips. Initially, it fails often (random attempts). But once it succeeds and gets a reward, it will try to repeat the motions that led to success, refining them to be more reliable. Eventually, it learns an efficient way to grasp objects. Google has done experiments with multiple robot arms learning in parallel and sharing their experience to speed up this kind of learning.

One more accessible example: **video game AI**. Some AIs have learned to play classic Atari games from scratch using reinforcement learning. The only input they get is the game screen pixels and the game score as a reward. The AI doesn't even know the rules initially; it just sees the screen and tries random controller inputs. But the game score acts as the reward signal. If pressing right makes the score go up (say a point for moving forward), it will eventually learn to favor pressing right. If falling in a pit resets the game (score didn't increase or went down), it will learn to avoid whatever led to that. Over many hours of play, these AIs often reach superhuman skill at those games, discovering how to exploit them for maximum points. For example, one famous result was an AI that learned to play **Breakout** (the game where you bounce a ball to break bricks). It eventually discovered a strategy to carve out a tunnel on one side and send the ball behind the wall of bricks to hit many bricks from the back, a known clever strategy – it wasn't told to do that; it found it because that strategy yields high

reward (lots of bricks broken)
unaligned.io.

It's worth noting that reinforcement learning, while powerful, can be tricky to get right. It often requires careful shaping of the reward function. If the reward is too sparse (like only at the end of a long episode), learning is slow because the agent doesn't get much guidance until the very end. If the reward isn't aligned with the real goal, the agent might find loopholes or unintended ways to maximize reward (a sort of "be careful what you wish for"). For example, a robot learning to walk that gets a reward for forward distance might learn to do weird hops or exploit simulation quirks if those give distance, rather than an elegant walk – unless we also reward smoothness or penalize unnatural motions. This aspect touches on AI safety where an RL agent might take unintended shortcuts to get reward, which in a real scenario might be undesirable (we'll touch on ethics later).

In summary, **reinforcement learning is learning from interaction and feedback (rewards)** rather than from examples or pure observation. It's the closest form of AI learning to the idea of an autonomous **agent** improving with experience, making it very relevant to robotics, game AI, and any scenario where an AI must make a sequence of decisions to achieve a goal. It is by trial and error, akin to how we often learn new tasks: try something, see what happens, and adjust.

*(Summary: Reinforcement learning involves an AI agent learning by trial and error through interactions with an environmentunaligned.io. The agent*

*takes actions and receives rewards (positive or negative feedback) based on the outcomes. Over time, it learns a strategy (policy) that maximizes its rewards. This is analogous to training a pet with treats for good behavior [unaligned.io](unaligned.io), or how humans learn many skills by gradually improving from feedback. RL has led to impressive results, like game-playing AIs that learn to win games by playing millions of rounds and discovering what strategies yield the highest score [theguardian.com](theguardian.com). It's a powerful approach for any problem where decision-making in a sequential process is needed. Next, we'll look at the concept of AI agents more generally, tying together how these learning methods allow an agent to perceive, decide, and act.)*

# Chapter 7: Deep Learning and Neural Networks – The Brain of Modern AI

Throughout our discussion of machine learning, we've mentioned neural networks and deep learning a few times. Deep learning has become one of the most important drivers of modern AI, powering everything from image recognition to voice assistants to self-driving cars. But what exactly is a **neural network**, and why do we call it "deep" learning?

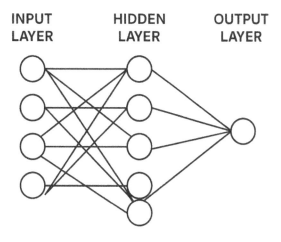

**INPUT LAYER**  **HIDDEN LAYER**  **OUTPUT LAYER**

A **neural network** is a type of machine learning model inspired (loosely) by the structure of the human brain ibm.com. In the brain, we have billions of interconnected neurons that transmit signals to each other, allowing us to process information and learn. An artificial neural network tries to mimic this with layers of interconnected "nodes" or "neurons." Each node is a simple processing unit that takes some input, applies a transformation (like a weighted sum plus an activation function), and passes output to the next layer. While each artificial neuron is very simplistic (certainly far simpler than a biological neuron), when you have thousands or millions of them connected in a network, the system can model very complex functions.

**Structure of a neural network:** The neurons are organized in layers:

- The **input layer** takes the raw data (for instance, pixel values of an image, or sensor readings, or features of an example).

- Then come one or more **hidden layers**, where each neuron in a layer takes inputs from many neurons in the previous layer, performs its little computation, and passes it on. Hidden layers are where the intermediate computations happen.

- Finally, an **output layer** produces the result (like probabilities for each class in classification, or a single number in regression).

If a network has many hidden layers (not just one or two, but potentially dozens or even hundreds), it is called a **deep neural network** – hence the term **deep learning**ibm.comibm.com. "Deep" refers to having multiple layers of depth in the network.

Why have multiple layers? Each layer of a neural network can be thought of as learning progressively more abstract features. For example, in an image recognition neural network:

- The first layer might look for very basic elements like edges or simple textures (because those are the smallest patterns in pixels).

- The next layer might take those edges and combine them into slightly more complex shapes or corners.

- A layer above that might recognize parts of objects (for instance, a neural net analyzing faces might have one layer that detects eyes, another that detects noses or mouths).

- The top hidden layers might combine those into recognizing a whole face. So by the time you reach the output layer, the network can say "this image is a face" or even "this is Alice's face." This hierarchy of features is a powerful aspect of deep learning. It **automatically learns representations** from raw data. In the past, a lot of work in AI involved manually engineering features (for example, someone might have had to program an algorithm to detect edges in images as a first step). Deep learning made it possible to learn those features directly from data, given enough examples and computational power.

Training a neural network is usually done by a supervised learning approach: you provide lots of examples with labels (like images with the identified object). The network initially has random weights (the strength of connections between neurons), so it makes random guesses. You compute the error (difference between its output and the correct output) and propagate that error backward through the network (this is aptly named **backpropagation**). The algorithm adjusts the weights slightly to reduce the error. By doing this over and over (often with stochastic gradient descent, which is a method to gradually adjust weights), the network's predictions get closer to the true labels. Essentially, the network "learns" the pattern that maps inputs to outputs, but internally what it's doing is adjusting all those connections between neurons so that, say, neurons in early layers respond to useful low-level features, neurons in later layers respond to higher-level concepts, etc. This learning process might involve millions of tiny adjustments (imagine tuning a huge number of knobs slightly until everything aligns).

One might ask: why did deep learning become so popular and effective? A couple of reasons:

- **Data**: We have much more data now (think of all the images, text, and user behavior data generated daily). Complex models like deep networks typically need a lot of data to reach their potential.

- **Computing Power**: Neural networks, especially deep ones, are computationally intensive. The rise of powerful GPUs (graphics processing units) and specialized hardware allowed training networks that were previously too slow or infeasible.

- **Algorithmic Advances**: Improvements in network architectures (like convolutional neural networks for images, recurrent networks for sequences, transformers for language, etc.) and training techniques made deep learning more practical and robust.

The result is that deep learning models have achieved astonishing performance in many tasks:

- In **image recognition**, deep neural networks surpassed human-level accuracy in certain benchmarks around the mid-2010s. That's why your phone can so reliably categorize photos or why services like Google Image search work so well. It's also why we suddenly have things like the "DeepArt" apps or filters that transform photos into paintings – neural networks can learn artistic styles and apply them (so-called generative deep learning).

- In **speech recognition**, deep learning allowed huge leaps. The voice assistants' ability to understand you is largely thanks to deep recurrent or convolutional networks trained on vast amounts of audio data. Same for real-time translation services.

- In **natural language processing (NLP)**, which deals with text, deep learning (particularly models called Transformers that led to systems like GPT) has dramatically improved language understanding and generation. That's how we have AI that can translate languages, summarize articles, or even generate text that reads quite coherently.

- **Playing complex games** like Go or StarCraft – those RL agents we talked about often use deep networks internally to approximate the "value" of positions or the best move (AlphaGo had deep neural networks guiding its play theguardian.com). The combination of reinforcement learning and deep learning is called deep reinforcement learning.

- **Driving**: Self-driving car prototypes use deep learning extensively – for instance, to interpret camera images (what objects are around, where are the lane lines, etc.) using convolutional neural networks.

To give a tangible sense of a neural network, consider a simplified example: **predicting student exam scores from study hours** (a toy regression problem). We might use a small network with 2 inputs (hours studied, hours slept perhaps), a hidden layer of, say, 3 neurons, and one output (predicted score). In the hidden layer, each neuron might take a weighted combo of [study, sleep] and output some intermediate feature like "preparedness level 1, 2, 3" with some non-linear activation (like neurons often use a function such as ReLU or sigmoid – details aside, it just introduces non-linearity which is important for modeling complex relations). These then feed into the output neuron that again combines them to get the final score prediction. During training, if a particular student's predicted score was too low compared to actual, the network adjusts weights: maybe it learns to weight "hours studied" more heavily. Another neuron might catch the diminishing returns of study (maybe too many hours without sleep is bad, etc.). In a small network, you might interpret what neurons do, but in a very large network (like hundreds of layers with thousands of neurons each, used in, say, image recognition), they become a bit of a black box with millions of parameters. However, researchers do try to interpret them; for images, they have visualized what patterns neurons respond to – some clearly fire for specific shapes or objects.

**Deep learning models** can sometimes even outperform humans in specific tasks (like radiology image screening in some studies, or finding patterns in data that are very high-dimensional). However, they also have weaknesses: they can be fooled by so-called adversarial examples (tiny changes in input that humans wouldn't notice can sometimes throw off a neural network drastically), and they often need a lot of data and computational resources to train. They also typically lack a degree of explainability – it's not always clear *why* a deep network made a certain decision, which can be a concern in fields like healthcare or finance.

There are various specialized network architectures:

- **Convolutional Neural Networks (CNNs)**: Great for images and spatial data, they use convolution operations to efficiently detect features like edges, textures, etc., in images. Think of it like scanning a filter over an image to find specific patterns. CNNs drive most image and video recognition tasks.

- **Recurrent Neural Networks (RNNs)** and their variant **LSTMs/GRUs**: Designed for sequence data like time series or text. They process one element at a time (like one word after another) and keep a sort of memory (internal state) that carries information along the sequence. These are used for language modeling, translation, and any time-order data.

- **Transformers**: A newer architecture (which powers models like GPT-3 or BERT) that has taken over NLP tasks. They handle sequences but more efficiently and capture long-range dependencies well, making them state-of-the-art for language and also being applied to other domains.

- **Autoencoders**: Networks that learn to compress data and then reconstruct it. Useful for unsupervised representation learning or tasks like noise reduction.

- **Generative Adversarial Networks (GANs)**: Two networks (a generator and a discriminator) pit against each other, one trying to create fake data (like realistic fake images) and the other trying to detect fakes. This has led to very realistic image generation (e.g., "deepfake" videos or AI-generated art).

- **Deep Reinforcement Learning**: Using deep networks as function approximators for value or policy in reinforcement learning tasks.

For a non-technical professional, the takeaway is: deep learning is a powerful subtype of machine learning that automatically learns features and representations from raw data by using multi-layer neural networks. It's why AI has become so good at perceptual tasks (seeing, hearing, translating language) in the last decade. It does, however, often require lots of data, and the models can be complex.

You might wonder, do you as a user interact with deep learning? Absolutely. When you use Google or Siri to transcribe your voice, a deep neural net is doing the speech recognition. When Facebook automatically tags friends in photos, that's a deep net recognizing faces. When Gmail suggests replies or categorizes mail, that's at least partially neural nets understanding language. Even when you use a banking app that detects potential fraud, behind the scenes there might be a neural net flagging unusual patterns.

One interesting development is **transfer learning** – where a neural network trained on one task is re-used (with some fine-tuning) for another task. For example, a neural network trained on millions of general images (like the ImageNet competition data) learns very general visual features. If you want to make a medical image classifier but you have limited medical images, you can take the pre-trained general network and fine-tune it on your specific images. Because it already knows how to detect edges, textures, etc., it only needs to adjust to the new domain, and you can get good performance with less data. This is widely used to adapt deep learning to specialized tasks without starting from scratch.

To recap: **deep learning** is essentially using neural networks with multiple layers to learn complex patterns from data. It's "deep" because of the many layers through which data gets transformed. These networks, with enough data, can achieve amazing feats – sometimes at the cost of being data-hungry and not easily interpretable. They form the basis of many advanced AI systems today.

*(Summary: Deep learning is a modern approach to AI that uses multi-layered neural networks to automatically learn representations from data ibm.com ibm.com. A neural network is inspired by the brain's interconnected neurons and can learn to recognize patterns like images, speech, or text by adjusting the strengths of connections based on training data. "Deep" networks have many layers, allowing them to learn simple features first and then build up to complex concepts. This method has driven major improvements in tasks such as image*

*recognition, speech recognition, and language understanding, because it can handle very complex patterns that would be hard to capture with manual rules. The downside is they often need a lot of data and act like a bit of a black box. Nonetheless, deep learning is a cornerstone of many AI applications today, often operating behind the scenes in the tools and apps we use.)*

# Chapter 8: AI Agents – Machines that Perceive, Reason, and Act

We've talked about different ways an AI can learn or be designed – supervised, unsupervised, reinforcement, deep learning – but let's zoom out and talk about the broader concept of an **AI agent**. An **AI agent** is essentially an entity (software, or a robot) that **perceives** its environment, **makes decisions**, and **takes actions** autonomously to achieve certain goals geeksforgeeks.org.

This idea is a key aspect of AI as a field. In fact, one way to define AI is by saying it's about creating **rational agents** – systems that act in a way to achieve the best expected outcome given their objectives and the

information they have
aws.amazon.com.

An AI agent can be:

- **Software-based**: like a chatbot, a recommendation engine, a virtual assistant, or even a piece of malware that propagates itself – anything that senses input (from user interactions, data streams, etc.) and acts (outputs a response, makes a change in a database, sends a message, etc.).

- **Embodied (robotic)**: like a robot vacuum, a self-driving car, a drone, a factory robot arm, etc., which sense the physical world with sensors and act with motors or other actuators.

The common thread is **autonomy**: an agent operates on its own (within its designed parameters). Humans set the goals or provide the environment, but the agent decides how to accomplish the goalsaws.amazon.com.

Let's break down an agent's key components and operation:

1. **Perception (Sensors)**: The agent has ways to perceive the state of the environment. For a software agent, "sensors" could be API calls, data inputs, or user inputs. For a physical agent, sensors are things like cameras, microphones, lidars, touch sensors, thermometers, etc. This perception gives the agent the **state** or context it's currently in.

2. **Decision Making (Brain)**: Based on what's perceived, the agent's AI "brain" decides what to do next. This decision could be rule-based (if A, then do B), or based

on a learned model (like a neural network deciding on steering angle for a self-driving car), or involve planning algorithms that simulate outcomes. In many cases, this is where the methods we discussed come in: a supervised model might be making a prediction to inform a decision, or a reinforcement learning policy might be selecting the next action.

3. **Action (Actuators)**: The agent then takes action to affect the environment. For a software agent, an action might be outputting a message, updating a database, sending an email, or recommending an item. For a robot, actions are physical moves: turning wheels, applying brakes, moving an arm, speaking via a speaker, etc.

4. **Environment**: The environment then changes (or remains) and produces new perceptions. This could include responses from users, changes in external data, or in the physical world scenario (e.g., the car moved to a new position on the road).

5. Loop back: The agent perceives the new state, and the cycle continues.

This loop is often called the **perception-action cycle**. In a sense, it's the AI equivalent of the human reflex loop: see world -> think -> act -> see new state -> ....

To illustrate, consider a **self-driving car** as an AI agent:

- It has sensors: cameras to see lanes, pedestrians, other cars; radar and lidar to sense distance; GPS and speed sensors.

- It has a goal: say, drive to a destination safely following traffic rules.

- Each moment, it perceives the environment: a curve ahead, a car in the next lane, a speed limit sign, etc.

- The decision-making component (a suite of AI models and control algorithms) processes these: maybe one module identifies objects (using deep learning on camera images), another predicts what nearby vehicles will do next, another plans an optimal path on the road, and another decides how to steer and accelerate right now. All these together decide the next actions: e.g., "slow down a bit and shift slightly to the right within the lane to maintain safe distance from that merging truck."

- Actions: it adjusts steering angle and throttle/brakes (actuators).

- The environment responds: the car moves, the sensors now see a slightly different scene (perhaps the truck is now safely ahead, etc.), and the cycle repeats continuously (dozens of times per second).

Now consider a **software agent** example: an AI-based **customer service chatbot** (like those that pop up on websites with "How can I help you?"):

- Perception: it "reads" the messages the user types (this is text input).

- Decision: its AI brain (NLP model) interprets the question and decides on the best answer or action. For simple ones, it might match keywords to FAQ answers (rule-based). Advanced ones use language understanding models to classify what the user needs and possibly query a database or use a knowledge base to formulate an answer. Some are powered by something akin to GPT behind the scenes to generate human-like responses.

- Action: it outputs a text answer or perhaps performs an action like "reset password" if the user requested that and it has the capability.

- The environment (the chat context) updates with the new

message. If the user asks a follow-up, the agent perceives that and so on.

What makes an agent "intelligent" is how well it can make those decisions – which is where all the AI techniques come in. A simple thermostat is a very basic agent (perceives temperature, if above threshold, turn off heater, else turn on – a fixed rule). We usually reserve the term "AI agent" for more complex and adaptive decision makers.

AI agents can also be **goal-driven or utility-driven**:

- **Goal-driven**: They aim to achieve a specific goal or set of goals. For example, an agent's goal might be "reach location X" or "maintain room temperature at 22°C". It will act in whatever way (within its allowed actions) to achieve that goal.

- **Utility-driven (rational)**: They have a utility function or reward that they try to maximize. This is essentially what reinforcement learning sets up: a reward (utility) that the agent accumulates; the agent's behavior is tuned to maximize that.

One important aspect is that agents often operate under uncertainty and have to handle unexpected situations. A well-designed AI agent should be able to adapt or at least handle a range of inputs. For example, a home cleaning robot should still function if it encounters a new type of chair it hasn't seen – maybe it tries a different path if it bumps into it. Or a trading agent in finance needs to adapt to market changes.

**Practical uses of AI agents**:

- **Virtual Personal Assistants** (Siri, Alexa, Google Assistant): These are agents that interact via conversation. They perceive voice commands, interpret them, maintain context, and take actions like answering queries, controlling smart home devices, or adding calendar events. They operate with the goal of helping the user accomplish tasks with voice. Under the hood, they incorporate many AI components: speech recognition (to perceive), NLP (to understand), decision logic (to choose actions/answers), sometimes short-term memory of context, and they act by responding or executing tasks (playing music, calling someone).

- **Autonomous Robots and Drones**: From vacuum cleaners to drones delivering packages to robots exploring Mars (like the Mars rovers). These are agents that often combine perception (via cameras, sensors) and decision-making for navigation and task execution. A Mars rover, for instance, has to autonomously plan a safe path to a target rock to sample, avoiding large boulders or steep slopes (since communication delay makes it impossible for humans to joystick in real-time). It uses its cameras (perception), on-board path planning algorithms (decision), and wheel actuators (action) to do this.

- **Game AI Agents**: The non-player characters (NPCs) in video games are agents. A simple Goomba in Mario that just walks forward is a very simplistic agent (no perception beyond maybe "did I hit a wall, if so turn around"). More advanced enemies might have state machines (patrol until player seen, then chase, etc.). In complex strategy games, AI opponents might gather resources, build units, attack or defend based on what the player does – these are agents making decisions to win the game.

- **Intelligent Web Agents**: These could include web crawlers that autonomously browse the web to index pages (like mini robots navigating hyperlinks), or AI scheduling assistants (like some services that can coordinate meeting times by emailing participants and finding a slot – they act like a human assistant in email conversations).

- **Industrial AI agents**: e.g., an AI system that monitors a manufacturing process and adjusts machine settings to optimize output or quality. It perceives via sensors on the production line, and acts by tuning knobs or alerting humans if needed. It may have a goal of maximizing throughput while minimizing defects, and it balances those via its decision-making.

- **Multi-agent systems**: Sometimes multiple AI agents interact. For instance, swarm of delivery drones cooperating to cover an area, or agents trading in a market, or simply multi-agent simulation used in training (like multiple RL agents playing against each other, which is how some strategies are learned).

What's critical with AI agents is they often need to handle the **unexpected** and make real-time decisions. An agent in the real world (like a self-driving car) can't possibly have been pre-programmed for every scenario (what if an ostrich runs across the highway? The car's AI likely never specifically saw that, but it should generalize from "any unexpected obstacle = slow/stop safely" rule). This is why combining sensing (like deep learning for object detection) with planning (maybe rule-based safety protocols) is common.

Another concept is **agent architecture** – some AI systems are designed with layers like:

- **Reactive layer**: for immediate responses (reflexes, like "brake if obstacle extremely close").

- **Deliberative layer**: for planning and reasoning longer term ("figure out a route to destination").

- **Learning component**: for improving over time (like updating its world model or refining its behavior based on experience). This is beyond our scope, but just know agents can be designed in modular ways to handle different levels of behavior.

It's also worth noting that not all AI agents learn continuously. Some might be deployed with a fixed policy learned during development. For instance, a factory robot might have a trained model for detecting objects and a fixed program for moving items – it doesn't learn on the fly, but it's still an autonomous agent. Others, like reinforcement learning agents in simulation, might continue to learn (some trading bots might adapt their strategies over time). For safety, a lot of deployed agents are mostly running learned or pre-programmed behaviors rather than learning in the wild, except for cases like online systems that update periodically or with reinforcement signals (maybe recommendation engines updating as more clicks are observed – they are agents that improve their recommendations as they get more data).

**Example scenario**: Consider a smart home **energy management agent**. It perceives information like current electricity pricing, whether the sun is out (if solar panels are installed), current energy usage, and possibly even weather forecasts. It has actions like turning on/off appliances or battery storage, adjusting thermostat setpoints, or drawing from the grid vs battery. Its goal is to minimize energy cost while keeping home comfortable. This agent might:

- At a time of day when electricity is expensive, decide to switch the water heater off for an hour to save cost, since the water is already hot enough.

- If solar panels are generating excess power, decide to charge the home battery.

- Sense the house is empty (maybe via security system sensors), so it can let the temperature drift a bit further from ideal (to save HVAC energy) until just before occupants return.

- All these decisions are autonomous, based on its programming or learned strategy. It perceives various sensor inputs, runs a decision algorithm (maybe an optimization model or learned policy), and acts by sending commands to devices. This improves efficiency without homeowner's constant input.

In summary, an AI agent is the holistic concept of an AI-driven autonomous entity that **perceives its environment, makes decisions, and takes actions towards a goal**aws.amazon.com. The learning methods we discussed (ML, RL, etc.) are like the tools that can give agents their decision-making smarts. When you put it all together – sensors + decision algorithms + actuators – you get an agent that can operate in the world or cyberspace to do something useful on its own.

*(Summary: An AI agent is an autonomous system (software or robot) that perceives its environment, decides what to do, and acts, all in pursuit of certain goals geeksforgeeks.orgaws.amazon.com. It's basically the "whole package" of AI in action: sensing (through data or sensors), reasoning (using AI models or logic), and acting (outputting a decision or physical action). Examples include self-driving cars (perceive*

road, decide steering/braking, act by controlling the vehicle), virtual assistants (listen to request, decide on answer, respond with action or info), and game AIs. AI agents operate in a perception-action loop, continually observing and responding. They can use the learning techniques we've discussed to improve their decisions. In the next chapter, we will shift focus to broader considerations: the ethical implications and limitations of AI, which apply to all these agents and systems we've talked about.)

# Chapter 9: Ethical Considerations and Limitations of AI

As powerful and exciting as AI is, it comes with important **ethical considerations and limitations** that we must address, especially as AI becomes more widespread in society. This chapter will discuss some key issues: bias and fairness, privacy, transparency, the limits of AI's capabilities, and the impacts on jobs and society. The goal is to highlight in a beginner-friendly way that AI is not magic or infallible – it's a human-created technology with strengths and weaknesses, and it carries certain risks if not used responsibly.

## 9.1 Bias and Fairness

One major concern with AI, particularly machine learning systems, is **bias**. Since ML models learn from data, they can inadvertently learn any biases present in that data upwork.com. If the training data reflects historical or societal biases, the AI may reproduce or even amplify those biases in its decisions. This can lead to unfair or discriminatory outcomes, even if there's no intent to discriminate.

For example, suppose a bank uses an AI model to help decide who gets loans. If historically the bank's data (whether due to societal bias or other factors) had more defaults among a certain group, the model might pick up on correlated features (like zip code, which can correlate with race or income) and end up unfairly denying loans to that group at a higher rate – essentially redlining via algorithm. This happened in a famous case with a hiring algorithm: **Amazon had an**

**experimental AI recruiting tool that became biased against women**. It learned from resumes the company had received over 10 years, most of which came from men (reflecting the male dominance in tech jobs). As a result, the AI started favoring male candidates and penalizing resumes that even contained the word "women's" (e.g., "women's chess club")reuters.com. Amazon had to scrap this tool once they realized it was discriminatingreuters.com.

Another example is facial recognition technology. Early facial recognition AIs had much higher error rates on non-white, especially darker-skinned, faces. Why? Often because the training sets were not diverse enough and were skewed toward lighter-skinned individuals. One widely cited test by a researcher (Joy Buolamwini) showed some systems failed to correctly recognize dark-skinned female faces up to 34% of the time while almost perfectly recognizing white male faces – a huge disparity. In one real-world incident, an AI-powered webcam was found to track white faces but not black faces because it had likely not been trained on diverse data (an example of inadvertent bias in product deployment). More gravely, a **facial recognition system used by law enforcement misidentified a black man as a suspect**, leading to a wrongful arrestupwork.com. The man was innocent; the AI had made an identification error potentially due to bias in how it recognized faces.

This illustrates **algorithmic bias**: if we're not careful, AI can perpetuate injustices present in data. That's why fairness in AI is a big area of focus now – researchers and practitioners are developing techniques to detect bias in models and mitigate it (like ensuring the model's error rates are similar across groups, or by training on balanced data, or by explicitly removing sensitive attributes when making decisions, etc.).

There's also the notion of **ethical AI** which involves making sure AI decisions align with human values and don't result in unfair treatment. It's crucial, for instance, that an AI used in criminal justice (like to recommend parole or bail decisions) is carefully audited for bias, because a biased model could deepen inequalities (imagine it gives harsher risk assessments to one race due to biased crime data – that would be unacceptable).

**Fairness** can be tricky – there are multiple definitions of fairness and sometimes they conflict (for example, equalizing false positive rates vs equalizing selection rates for groups – a model can't always satisfy all criteria simultaneouslyvox.com). But the key takeaway is, AI is not inherently neutral or objective just because it's math. It learns from us, so it can pick up our prejudices unless actively checked.

## 9.2 Privacy and Data Protection

AI systems often rely on large amounts of data, some of which can be personal or sensitive. This raises **privacy concerns**upwork.com. For instance:

- Voice assistants are always listening for the wake word, which means they have a microphone on in your home. People have worried about what data is recorded and how it's used. There have been incidents where Alexa or Google Assistant mistakenly thought it was triggered and recorded private conversations.

- Apps on your phone using AI might track your usage patterns, locations, habits (to make recommendations, etc.). That data, if mishandled or breached, can expose a lot about you.

- Face recognition cameras in public can be used to identify and track individuals, which feels invasive and can be a tool for mass surveillance if abused. Some cities have banned or limited facial recognition use by authorities for this reason.

- AI models trained on personal data could inadvertently memorize parts of the data. A trivial example: an AI trained on a dataset of customer info might accidentally spit out a real person's phone number if prompted in the wrong way, because it effectively learned it. This is a concern especially for those big language models that were trained on internet text – people have found they sometimes can output things like someone's contact info or code that was in the training data, which they arguably shouldn't reveal.

**Data privacy** regulations like GDPR in Europe emphasize that personal data should be used with consent and for specific purposes. If companies want to leverage AI on user data, they must ensure compliance – e.g., anonymizing data, allowing users to opt out, deleting data upon request, etc.

A real scenario highlighting privacy issues: In 2018, a fitness tracking app (Strava) released a global heatmap of users' runs. Unexpectedly, this inadvertently revealed the locations of secret military bases, because soldiers jogging on bases created heat trails on the map. The AI here was simple (just aggregating GPS), but it shows how data, when processed and made public even unintentionally, can have serious privacy implications.

Another privacy example touched in Chapter 3: employees feeding sensitive info into ChatGPT and not realizing it might be stored. Indeed, **Samsung engineers accidentally leaked confidential data to ChatGPT** when they used it to help debug code upwork.com. That data potentially becomes part of ChatGPT's training data or at least sits on OpenAI's servers, creating a data security risk.

After that, Samsung limited usage of external AI tools by employees.

So, confidentiality of data used in AI is crucial. If an AI service is cloud-based, using it might mean sending data to a third-party server, which must be trusted and secure.

There's also **personal privacy** in how AI is used: say an insurance company uses an AI that monitors your driving (via an app) to set your rates. That's convenient, but you might feel uncomfortable being monitored constantly, even if you're a good driver. If AI is used in hiring, it might analyze your social media or video interviews for traits – which can feel invasive or like a privacy violation if not transparent.

## 9.3 Transparency and Explainability

Many AI systems, especially deep learning models, are like **"black boxes"** – they make decisions in ways that are not easily interpretable by humansupwork.com. While high accuracy is great, in sensitive applications we also want to know **why** the AI made a decision. This is the field of **AI explainability** or XAI.

For example, if an AI medical diagnosis system says "This patient has disease X," the doctor will want to know what evidence the AI saw to reach that conclusion (was it a shadow on an X-ray? Some combination of lab results?). If the AI can't explain itself, the doctor might not trust it or know how to act on it. Or consider a loan applicant denied by an AI model – under regulations like GDPR, individuals have a right to an explanation of decisions made about them. The bank would need to provide an understandable reason like "your income was below threshold" or "you have a short credit history," rather than just "our algorithm said no."

This ties into **accountability**: if an AI makes a mistake, who is responsible? How do we audit it? Transparency helps here – knowing the factors influencing decisions can help identify if something went wrong (like the model used an inappropriate factor such as race, or simply that it had a bug).

Various techniques are being used to improve explainability:

- Simpler models (where feasible) like decision trees or rule-based systems are inherently more interpretable ("if condition A and B, then yes" is easy to follow).

- For complex models, add-on tools like LIME or SHAP can highlight which features were most important in a particular decision (e.g., for an image classifier, highlight which parts of the image contributed to classifying it as, say, "dog" – maybe the ear shape).

- Some deep learning research tries to build interpretability in, or at least visualize what neurons are looking for.

**The "black box" problem**: especially in fields like finance or healthcare, there's a hesitation to deploy completely black-box models. One compromise is using them as advisors but having humans in the loop for final decisions. For instance, a "black box" AI might flag certain transactions as likely fraud, but then a human analyst reviews those flags rather than automatically blocking accounts. The human might catch if the AI's rationale was flawed, but at least the AI helps narrow down cases.

Transparency also extends to users knowing when they are interacting with AI. Some jurisdictions propose that if you're talking to a chatbot or an AI-generated text/image, it should be disclosed. Deepfake technology (AI-generated realistic audio/video) raised alarms – to combat potential misuse (like fake news, impersonations) there's talk about watermarking AI-generated content or other ways to identify it.

## 9.4 Safety and Reliability

AI systems, especially in high-stakes domains (transportation, healthcare, etc.), must be **reliable and safe**. They should handle edge cases gracefully and fail safely if needed. For example, a self-driving car's AI should be designed with multiple redundancies (if the main vision system fails, perhaps a backup system can take over or the car can safely slow down and stop). We have to consider worst-case scenarios: what if the AI encounters a scenario it wasn't trained for? In 2016, a fatal accident occurred with a semi-autonomous car (Tesla on Autopilot) because the system failed to recognize the side of a white truck against a bright sky; it didn't brake and the car went under the truck. That showed the limitation – the image recognition failed in an edge case. Since then improvements have been made, but it underlines that AI has limits in perception.

**Generalization** is a limitation: AI models can perform very well on data similar to what they saw in training, but they can struggle with data that's outside that distribution. If something very new or rare happens, an AI might mispredict. Humans, with common sense, might adapt better to novel situations (though not always).

Another limitation: **lack of common sense and context understanding**. AI can seem to understand, especially advanced language models, but they don't truly have human-like understanding. They don't have consciousness or true comprehension of meaning; they pattern-match based on training data. This leads to situations where an AI might give an answer that sounds plausible but is completely wrong or nonsensical if you really think about it. These are often called "AI hallucinations" in generative models – confidently stating false information. For critical applications, this is a big limitation; you can't fully trust an answer just because it's from an AI, you might need verification.

AI also lacks **human qualities like empathy** (unless explicitly mimicked) and judgment that goes beyond data. An AI might not understand moral or social implications unless those are somehow encoded. For instance, a content filter AI might block something that is actually satire or educational, because it sees "bad" keywords. It doesn't "get the joke" or context unless it's trained deeply on context and even then, nuance is hard.

In terms of learning, many AI systems require **lots of data and compute** (especially deep learning). That can be a practical limitation – you might not have enough data to train an effective model for a niche task. Also, training big models consumes significant energy (there's an environmental impact aspect; large AI models can have a carbon footprint, which is a consideration ethically for sustainability).

## 9.5 Impact on Employment and Society

AI's increasing capabilities naturally raise questions about **job displacement**. This is a broad societal consideration: will AI automate tasks faster than new jobs are created, and how do we transition the workforce? Historically, technology has both eliminated some jobs and created new ones, and overall productivity rises. With AI, some roles that involve routine cognitive work (like entry-level accounting or certain back-office tasks) might be streamlined by AI. For example, AI can now draft basic legal documents or analyze contracts, which might reduce the need for as many junior lawyers for those tasks upwork.com. AI customer service bots might handle many inquiries that human agents used to handle, affecting call center jobs.

However, new roles are emerging too – for instance, the need for AI maintenance, oversight, data labeling, etc., and jobs that involve what AI can't do well: strategic thinking, complex human interaction, creativity that requires understanding human culture at a deep level, etc.

Many experts believe the nature of many jobs will change rather than wholesale disappear in the short term. Humans might work alongside AI (e.g., a doctor with AI diagnostic tools, or a marketer using AI to analyze consumer data then coming up with a campaign). But it is important as a society to prepare for shifts – through education and retraining programs, for example – to ensure people can move into roles that AI augments rather than competes with.

Another social impact is **dependency and skill loss**: If we rely too much on AI for tasks, do we lose human expertise? For example, if doctors over-rely on AI diagnoses, could their diagnostic skills atrophy? Or if drivers rely on GPS and self-driving, do they lose their own navigation skills? This might not be a huge concern if AI is consistently reliable, but if the AI fails and humans have lost practice, that could be problematic.

**Misuse of AI**: Any powerful tool can be misused. Deepfakes (AI-generated fake videos) can be used maliciously to spread false information or for personal revenge (like fake videos to harass someone). AI can be used by bad actors – e.g., to automate hacking (finding vulnerabilities via AI), or to create extremely convincing phishing messages personalized via AI. The ethics community often talks about AI safety in terms of not just accidents but intentional misuse. That's why there are also efforts to set norms and possibly regulations around certain applications (like banning autonomous lethal weapons – the idea of AI deciding to target/kill without human oversight is something many argue should be off-limits).

**Accountability and Legal Frameworks**: If an AI causes harm (like a self-driving car in an accident), legal frameworks are still catching up. Who is liable – the manufacturer, the owner, the software developer? This is being debated and will shape how companies approach AI deployment. Clearer guidelines and laws can help ensure companies build AI with safety in mind from the get-go (since they might otherwise face liability).

**Ethical AI principles**: Many organizations have drafted principles or guidelines for AI ethics. Common themes:

- **Fairness**: Avoid bias, ensure equitable treatment upwork.com.

- **Transparency**: Be clear when people are interacting with AI and explain decisions where appropriateupwork.com.

- **Accountability**: Have human oversight and the ability to audit and correct AI behavior.

- **Privacy**: Protect user data and use it responsiblyupwork.com.

- **Beneficence**: AI should ideally benefit people and not cause harm (like "do no harm" for AI).

- **Freedom from misuse**: Don't develop AI for unlawful or unethical uses.

These are high-level, but companies like Google, Microsoft, etc., have internal AI ethics boards to evaluate projects (e.g., Google infamously decided not to continue a Pentagon AI contract after employee protests about it possibly being used for targeting in warfare).

In conclusion, while AI holds tremendous promise, it is not without pitfalls. Being aware of these issues is the first step to addressing them. Engineers need to deliberately design AI systems to mitigate bias, protect privacy, and behave transparently and safely. Policymakers and leaders need to create frameworks that ensure AI's benefits are broadly shared and its risks managed. And as users or professionals, we should remain thoughtful about how we deploy AI – asking not just "Can we do this with AI?" but "Should we, and how do we do it responsibly?"

*(Summary: AI is powerful but not perfect. It can unintentionally incorporate biases present in training data, leading to unfair outcomes if not checked[reuters.com](reuters.com). It raises privacy issues because it often uses personal data[upwork.com](upwork.com) – we must ensure data is handled properly and individuals' privacy is respected. Many AI models are black boxes, so there's a push for transparency and explainability to build trust and accountability[upwork.com](upwork.com). AI systems have technical limitations – they can make mistakes, especially outside of*

*their training scenarios, and they lack true common sense or human insight. We also face societal questions: how will AI impact jobs, and how do we prevent misuse of AI (like deepfakes or biased policing tools)? The key is to approach AI development and deployment with ethical principles in mind – fairness, privacy, transparency, safety – and to use human judgment as a complement. In the final chapter, we'll wrap up our discussion and reflect on the journey we've taken through AI and ML in this book.)*

# Chapter 10: Conclusion – Embracing AI with Understanding and Responsibility

Over the course of this book, we've traveled from the basic concepts of artificial intelligence and machine learning all the way through real-world applications, types of learning, AI agents, and the ethical landscape. By now, you should have a clear understanding of what AI is (and isn't), how machines learn from data, and how these technologies are already shaping the world around us in big and small ways.

Let's recap some key takeaways:

- **Artificial Intelligence** is about machines performing tasks that typically require human intelligence, such as understanding language, recognizing patterns, or making decisions iotforall.com. It ranges from simple rule-based systems to complex learning algorithms that improve themselves.

- **Machine Learning** is the engine of modern AI. Instead of programming every rule, we give machines data and they figure out the rules or patterns ibm.com. We covered supervised learning (learning from labeled examples, like a student with an answer key), unsupervised learning (finding hidden structure in unlabeled data, like discovering groupings), and reinforcement learning (learning by trial and error with rewards, like training a pet) unaligned.io.

- **Everyday AI**: We saw many examples of AI in action – from Netflix recommendations to Siri's voice recognition to Facebook's content filtering. AI is ubiquitous, often improving convenience and efficiency. But now you know that behind each of those conveniences is a specific type of model or algorithm doing the work (perhaps a neural network identifying your face in a photo, or a clustering algorithm grouping your shopping preferences).

- **AI Agents**: We combined it all to understand AI agents as autonomous entities that perceive their environment, decide, and act aws.amazon.com. Whether it's a software bot chatting with customers or a self-driving car navigating traffic, they are systems making choices using AI techniques. An agent might use supervised models for perception (like object detection), planning algorithms (maybe search or optimization), and even reinforcement learning for decision policies. AI agents are how AI becomes an actor in the real world.

- **Deep Learning**: We delved into neural networks and deep learning – the technology that has significantly advanced AI's capabilities in the last decade ibm.com. By layering many "neurons," deep learning systems automatically learn features and can achieve high performance in complex tasks like image and speech recognition. We demystified terms like neural networks, explaining they're essentially function approximators with many parameters that we train on data. You also learned why deep learning needs lots of data and computing power, and why it's considered a "black box" in many cases.

- **Ethics and Limitations**: Importantly, we discussed that AI is not without challenges. Bias in data can lead to biased AI reuters.com. Privacy must be safeguarded when AI uses personal dataupwork.com. We need transparency to trust AI decisions, especially in critical areasupwork.com. AI models can make errors, sometimes in unpredictable ways, and they generally lack the full breadth of human common sense. Moreover, AI's impact on jobs and society requires proactive thinking – re-skilling workers, setting ethical guidelines, and maybe regulatory guardrails to ensure AI is used for good and with minimal harm.

As a professional from a non-technical background, you might be wondering, "What does all this mean for me, and how can I leverage this knowledge?" Here are a few concluding thoughts in that direction:

- **AI as a Tool**: Think of AI not as a human replacement, but as a powerful tool. Just like spreadsheets or the internet, it's a tool that can augment what you do. With the concepts you've learned, you can identify areas in your domain where AI might help. For example, if you're in marketing, you now understand how an AI might segment customers or predict churn. If you're in healthcare administration, you see how AI could help triage patient inquiries or flag anomalies in billing. You don't need to build the model yourself, but you can be the idea person who spots the opportunity and works with technical teams to implement it.

- **Informed Decision-Making**: When vendors or colleagues talk about AI solutions, you can cut through the hype. You'll know the right questions to ask: Where is the training data coming from? Is this a supervised model – and if so, what labels was it trained on? How do we know it's accurate? Has it been tested for bias? What's the plan if it makes a wrong prediction? These questions will help ensure that AI projects in your organization are grounded in reality and responsibility.

- **Continuous Learning**: AI is a fast-evolving field. Today's state-of-the-art may change in a couple of years. But the fundamentals you learned here will remain useful. If you want to dive deeper, you could explore some beginner-friendly courses or resources on AI and ML (many are available online for free). You could even try out simple ML yourself using user-friendly tools (some AI platforms let you drag-and-drop data and train basic models without coding). Actually seeing a model learn from data – even a simple one – can reinforce these concepts and make them more concrete.

- **Collaboration with AI experts**: With your understanding, you can effectively bridge between technical teams and business teams. Often projects fail not because the tech doesn't work, but because of miscommunication – maybe the business expected magic, or the engineers optimized the wrong metric. You can help align goals, interpret results, and translate needs. For instance, you could help define what "success" means for an AI project in your context (is it reducing customer wait time by 50% using a chatbot? improving sales conversions by 10% through better recommendations?). Being specific and aligned on objectives and limitations is crucial.

- **Ethical Leadership**: No matter your role, advocating for ethical use of AI is important. If your company wants to implement an AI solution, ensure there's consideration of fairness, privacy, and accountability. If you spot a potential for bias or harm, raise it. Non-technical professionals often are closer to end-users or the societal context of a product, so your perspective is valuable to ensure AI is used appropriately. For example, if marketing suggests using an AI to analyze employees' facial expressions for "mood scoring" (there have been such proposals), you might point out the privacy invasion and dubious scientific basis – perhaps steering toward a more respectful solution.

Finally, it's worth expressing that while AI can seem like a buzzword, at its core it's a collection of tools and methods created by people to serve people. It's not some sentient entity or magic box (at least not with current technology!). AI has strengths – like handling huge volumes of data and finding patterns – and weaknesses – like understanding nuance or causality in the way humans do. The best outcomes often come from combining AI with human intelligence, each compensating for the other's shortcomings. For example, an AI model might sift through millions of medical records to find patterns indicating a rare disease, but human doctors will validate the findings and apply judgment to individual cases.

By embracing AI with both enthusiasm and caution, you can be part of shaping an "augmented" workforce where mundane tasks are automated and humans are freed to focus on what we do best: creative thinking, complex problem-solving, empathy, and strategic decision-making. The future of AI is really about how we choose to use it. With the knowledge you've gained, you're better equipped to make those choices wisely.

**Closing thought:** AI is often called a "general-purpose technology" like electricity or the internet – it has the potential to impact nearly every sector and aspect of life. Understanding it is becoming a key literacy of the 21st century. As you continue your journey, remember that AI is a tool created by us – it learns from the data we give it and the objectives we set. In that sense, the responsibility lies with us to ensure it's used to create positive outcomes. Equipped with understanding, you can help demystify AI for others and lead or contribute to projects that leverage AI in meaningful, ethical ways. The world of AI is evolving quickly, and it's an exciting time to be engaged with it. Stay curious, keep learning, and don't hesitate to collaborate with experts – the fusion of domain expertise (which you have) and AI know-how can lead to powerful innovations.